| | |
|---|---|
| 1 | Foreword |
| 3 | Touching the Past |
| 4 | Liangzhu Culture: A Story Etched in Jade |
| 8 | Hangzhou History Begins |
| 12 | Lady of the West |
| 14 | Rise of the City on the Lake |
| 16 | Aqueduct of Ages |
| 23 | Hangzhou's Protector |
| 26 | Glowing with Leifeng |
| 28 | The Legend of the White Snake |
| 31 | Dawn of the Southern Song |
| 35 | Discover Song Porcelain |
| 37 | West Lake, History, and Tomorrow |
| 39 | Marco Polo's City of Heaven |
| 42 | The Butterfly Effect at Wansong Academy |
| 45 | Historical Hotspots |
| 50 | Appendix |

专业外教　英文朗读
扫码免费收听全书

更多英文原创中国故事
来《汉语世界》畅读
theworldofchinese.com

注册网站，点击右上角 subscribe 订阅，
输入优惠码 HANGZHOU
享受读者专属折扣！

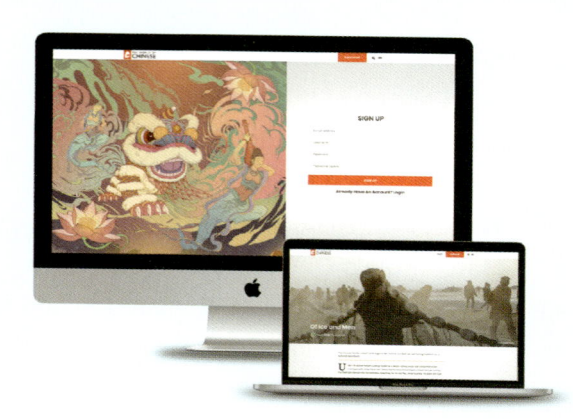

# Foreword

Hangzhou is a city of choices. You might find yourself past the Leifeng Pagoda first built in the 10th century, possibly looking at the Qianjiang CBD on your way to work. You could wake one morning as a nature lover eager to see birds on West Lake. Or you may be anxious to see the sites and walk the paths of hermits and pilgrims. Perhaps you would just like to have a cup of tea and watch lotus flowers. Hangzhou is not just one kind of city.

This guide helps travelers and residents find what they need for who they are, a handbook of travel stories from experienced writers and journalists with helpful hints, and appendixes. This guide fully serves Hangzhou's reputation as a city of stories and the very beginning of civilization. This guide has all the information you need.

Whether you're traveling to the Xixi Wetlands for viewing flowers, enjoying the 1,500-year-old Grand Canal, or thinking about a mortal man and a snake demon walking along West Lake, the quiet reflections of lakes, canals, and streams will follow you everywhere.

CBD
中央商务区

hermit
隐士

pilgrim
朝圣者

resident
居民

hint
提示

mortal man
凡人

demon
妖

reflection
倒影

杭州一瞥：访古探幽

**booming**
繁荣的

**hub**
中心

**entrepreneur**
企业家

**philosopher**
哲学家

Hangzhou is a city for all your holiday purposes. On the one hand, Hangzhou is a modern city of Alibaba, the G20, and a booming business hub; on the other, it's mountain streams, bamboo fields, and temples. Poets, entrepreneurs, travelers, hermits and philosophers—all found something in this ancient city. Hangzhou is a home for most people.

## Touching the Past

In Hangzhou, there are myths, legends, and stories. But, the best part about Hangzhou is that you can touch it. Young lovers can stand on the Broken Bridge and think of the great White Snake and the demon's eternal love. Pilgrims can climb the Leifeng Pagoda and imagine themselves king of the Wuyue Kingdom. Ambitious young writers can walk the path to the mausoleum of warrior poet Yue Fei and imagine themselves fighting off the Jurchen invaders. Travelers to Hangzhou's northwest Liangzhu can look back 5,000 years to the very beginning of civilization itself. Since those ancient days of porcelain and jade, Hangzhou has stimulated change, success, ups and downs of imperial politics as well as the likes of Marco Polo and Ibn Battuta, who saw a city so beautiful that they left words and essays behind. Brutal and benevolent rulers walked on the shores of West Lake, empires like the Southern Song rose and fell, and travelers around the world came to seek their fortune only to find their home here in Hangzhou.

myth
神话

eternal
永恒的

ambitious
有雄心的

mausoleum
陵墓

warrior
勇士

Jurchen
女真

invader
侵略者

porcelain
瓷器

jade
玉器

stimulate
激发

ups and downs
盛衰

imperial
帝国的

brutal
残暴的

benevolent
善良的

# Liangzhu Culture: A Story Etched in Jade

China has 5,000 years of history and the most powerful argument in favor of the claim lies in the Yuhang District, northwest of Hangzhou, in Liangzhu. There, amid well-preserved jade relics, one can find clues to an ancient Chinese civilization.

Liangzhu Culture, a Neolithic civilization about 5,300 and 4,500 years ago, was almost at the time of the Egyptian pharaohs.

## Liangzhu Museum

The Liangzhu Museum is the best place to catch a glimpse of the Liangzhu Culture. The museum itself is an impressive building, with limestone walls and Brutalist architecture. Within the museum and around the courtyard, visitors can learn about this ancient culture, believed to have been the first to use jade as a marker of social status.

Viewing the exhibits, keep an eye out for info on the key relics. Without a doubt the most important and eye-catching of them all is a very Chinese

---

well-preserved
保存完好的

relic
遗迹

Neolithic
新石器时代的

pharaoh
法老

glimpse
一瞥

limestone
石灰岩

Brutalist
粗野主义

courtyard
庭院

info
(information 缩略语) 信息

without a doubt
无疑

royal emblem.

The emblem was found at the Fanshan Hill site, which has a lot of tombs for the highest-ranking aristocrats of Liangzhu society, as evidenced by the quantity and quality of jade, being the signifier of social status.

Experts have different interpretations of the royal jade emblem. However, they tend to agree that this emblem was held by the king of a society that stretched from Sichuan in the southwest, Guangdong in the southeast, Qinghai and Gansu in the west, and Shaanxi and Shanxi in the north.

The unifying characteristics of the jade relics are rather clear. Jade *cong* and *bi* (tube and ring shaped ritual objects respectively) are of the greatest number.

## Day-to-Day Life of Liangzhu Culture

Seemingly, the seat of power for this society was the Liangzhu Ancient City; around the city walls, there are a number of dig sites still operating. At these dig sites, pieces of pottery from thousands of years ago are still regularly found. At one site, a nearby house was operated as a makeshift archaeological storage and classification area.

emblem
徽章

aristocrat
贵族

signifier
记号

interpretation
解释

stretch
延伸

unifying
统一的

*cong*
琮

*bi*
璧

ritual object
礼器

day-to-day
日复一日的

makeshift
临时的

archaeological
考古学的

classification
分类

| | |
|---|---|
| earthen terrace 土台 | |
| privilege 特权 | |
| farming implement 农具 | |
| engage in 参与 | |
| agricultural 农业的 | |
| thatched 茅草覆盖的 | |
| mud-hut 泥棚 | |
| log 圆木 | |
| straw 稻草 | |
| legacy 遗产 | |
| persist 持续 | |
| glance at 浏览 | |

The ancient city was about 1.9 kilometers long, from wall to wall, and 1.7 kilometers wide. The walls were thick, with their foundation ranging between 40 to 60 meters.

Little is known of the day-to-day workings of the city. Earthen terraces indicate a likely spot for a palace. The museum's exhibits do reveal some differences of daily life in this ancient culture. Although aristocrats enjoyed certain privilege in society, men were still buried with farming implements, indicating that even upper classes perhaps had to engage in farming to live on, which meant it was an early stage agricultural society. Farming played a big role in daily life, and most houses are believed to have been basic thatched mud-huts, built with logs and straw. The wide use of jade implements indicates that the culture had spread quite far, meaning there was probably trade among various communities.

The key aspect of Liangzhu Culture—its legacy of jade as an important marker of social status—has persisted throughout Chinese history, with jade a prized resource even today. So when glancing at jade items today, spare a thought for the ancient culture from which its attraction may have originated.

## Kuahuqiao Culture

Chinese historians regard Liangzhu Culture as one of the earliest forms of Chinese civilization, but the Hangzhou area was home to other cultures before this time. Kuahuqiao Culture, for example, is believed to have existed as a separate culture in modern day Hangzhou's southern Xiaoshan District by Xianghu Lake around 7,700 years ago. Little is known about this culture, but some archaeologists believe there is strong evidence to indicate the Kuahuqiao Culture was able to cultivate paddy rice using flooding and irrigation.

Here, the earliest canoe relic in China was also excavated. To learn more about the culture, visit the Kuahuqiao Site Museum.

historian
历史学家

archaeologist
考古学家

paddy rice
水稻

irrigation
灌溉

canoe
独木舟

excavate
挖掘

# Hangzhou History Begins

be famed for
以……著名

marsh
沼泽

tribal leader
部落领袖

disembark
上岸

roughly
大致

ferry
渡船

mythical
神话的

testimony
证据

The name Hangzhou began with a legend: about 4,000 years ago, Yu the Great, who started dynastic rule in China and who was famed for controlling the flooding of the Yellow River, went by boat through the marshes and wetlands to meet with other tribal leaders on Kuaiji Hill (present day Shaoxing City, 70 kilometers southeast of Hangzhou). He disembarked somewhere in modern day Hangzhou and people later called the spot "Yu Hang," roughly meaning "Yu's Ferry." Of course, modern scholars have varied interpretations of the events. Regardless of its mythical beginnings, the character "*hang*" remains in Hangzhou, a testimony to its watery past. Also, today a northwestern district of Hangzhou is named Yuhang, where you can visit the oldest civilization in the area, the Liangzhu site.

Far from the center of power, Hangzhou fell under the control of different states. In the rise of the first emperor in China, Qin Shi Huang, the city had a name in 222 BCE: Qiantang

County. That first emperor even followed the footsteps of Yu the Great on the way to the Kuaiji Hill to pay his respects. Legend has it that, in order to avoid stormy weather at sea, the emperor moored his boat to a rock, which was later carved into a Buddha statue. As the waterline has gradually receded, a temple was built around this statue, found today on Baoshi Hill north of West Lake.

Hangzhou's legendary body of water, West Lake, also took form during these long early centuries. Eastern Han Dynasty (25 – 220) official Hua Xin built the first ever dam to protect against the rising tide. Hua had a creative idea of motivating local residents to participate in this project by promising that anyone who delivered stone and dirt to the site would be paid a considerable amount of money, causing a delivery rush within days. He then declared there was no payment for the latecomers. Those late to the party were angry, but what could they do but empty the stone and dirt at the site? In this way, a dam was born.

---

moor
停泊

carve
雕刻

Buddha statue
佛像

waterline
吃水线

recede
退潮

legendary
传奇的

considerable
相当大的

latecomer
新来者

杭州一瞥：访古探幽

HANGZHOU HISTORIANS

View of West Lake featuring Baochu Pagoda
from atop Baoshi Hill north of the lake

# Lady of the West

take revenge on
复仇

conqueror
征服者

conquer
征服

hostage
人质

court
宫廷

humiliation
耻辱

stool
粪便

diagnosis
诊断

plot
阴谋

concubine
妾

Her name was Xishi, also known as Xizi, or the Lady of the West. A great poet once compared West Lake on a sunny day to her beauty, calling it Xizi Lake, named for the beautiful spy of the fifth century BCE who would take revenge on her homeland's conqueror.

States fought each other during the Spring and Autumn Period (770 BCE – 476 BCE), and Xishi was born a common village girl in the Yue State not far from Hangzhou. Her land was conquered by the State of Wu; her king, Goujian, was taken hostage and shamed in the enemy court.

Her beauty soon became so famous that fate came knocking. King Goujian returned after three years of disgrace and humiliation, but he managed to earn the trust of his enemy King Fuchai of Wu. At one point, Goujian even offered to taste the stool of Fuchai when he was sick to help the doctor with the diagnosis, but actually had a cold plot of revenge. Xishi, trained in music, dancing and fashion, has transformed from a simple village girl to a royal concubine who was selected by Goujian as a honey trap to distract Fuchai from state affairs. Unsurprisingly, Fuchai was enthralled by Xishi, having palaces built for her, going on trips with her, and ignoring the warnings of his wise minister Wu Zixu, even forcing him to commit suicide. Goujian, meanwhile, would sleep on a pile of firewood and taste animal bile every day to remind himself of the bitterness of revenge. He took time only to develop the economy and strengthen his troops. When battle came, Fuchai, who indulged in nothing but pleasure, lost everything including his life.

And what of Xishi? One ending tells of her living a life of peace and freedom with an official of Goujian's court. Thus ends the tale of the Lady of the West.

---

honey trap
美人计

distract
使分心

state affair
国家大事

enthrall
迷惑

commit suicide
自杀

bile
胆汁

bitterness
苦涩

indulge in
沉迷于

# Rise of the City on the Lake

West Lake's fate rose sharply during the Sui Dynasty (581 – 618) when the city was heavily taxed due to being designated the southernmost terminus of the Grand Canal.

The Grand Canal connected the east-west running Yangtze and Yellow rivers, creating a powerful commercial and cultural artery that transformed Chinese, Asian, and world history. Through networks of rivers and lakes, Hangzhou was connected to the interior of southern China down to the Pearl River and into the South China Sea.

After the Sui fell, early policies of the Tang (618 – 907) saw Hangzhou reap the benefits of Asian trade from Vietnam to Korea and from Japan to Central Asia. In 628, Emperor Taizong of Tang began to make three key policies of prosperity: the equal-field system, imperial examinations, and maintenance of communication and transportation infrastructure. Combined with the equal-field system, a new fast-ripening rice produced massive crops in southern China which flowed from Hangzhou to the north, with other southern goods like silk and pottery.

---

designate
指定为

terminus
终点

artery
干道

reap
收获

equal-field system
均田制

imperial examinations
科举考试

maintenance
维护

infrastructure
基础设施

Two key governors of Hangzhou during this time made the city more prosperous. One was named Li Bi, appointed in 781. Under his watch, clay and bamboo-pipe irrigation systems drew water out of West Lake, then at over 10 square kilometers, allowing the thirsty city to further flourish. The only remaining relic of his six wells is Xiangguo Well on Jiefang Road not far from West Lake.

Between 822 and 824, the famous poet and administrator Bai Juyi governed Hangzhou. By the time Bai arrived, the local dike was broken and fields were lack of water. He ordered to have a stronger and taller dike erected to control the water flow. Thanks to Bai, the farms became ripe with crops once again and the city blossomed. Many mistake the Bai Causeway on the north of the lake linking the Gushan Hill and northeastern shore as one of Bai Juyi's civic projects, but it was already there in Bai's time having a different name, "White Sand Causeway," or "Baisha Causeway." In honor of Bai Juyi, the causeway's name was later changed to "Bai Causeway."

When Bai left Hangzhou, West Lake was at its historical apex.

---

governor
地方长官

appoint
任命

clay
黏土

dike
堤坝

erect
使竖起

ripe
成熟

blossom
兴旺

civic project
市政工程

in honor of
向……表示敬意

apex
顶点

## Aqueduct of Ages

aqueduct
沟渠

Baxia
蚆蝮

arch
拱形

steer
操控

barge
驳船

integrate
整合

The four Baxia creatures guarding the main arch of Gongchen Bridge, legendary statues of the sons of the Dragon Emperor in Chinese mythology, look a bit nervous as their function is to stop unsteadily steered ships from hitting the bridge with nearly 400 years of history. However, in the past decade, those Baxia have been hit many times by heavy coal barges and stone barges in the Grand Canal. Ignoring the occasional crash, these creatures have seen the best of Chinese history pass to and from one of the greatest cities in ancient China.

To some, the Grand Canal may seem like an ordinary river, but in history it was once the heart of the global economy. Stretching nearly 1,800 kilometers from Beijing to Hangzhou, the Grand Canal integrated southern and northern China more than 1,400 years ago and it brought prosperity and communication.

The Grand Canal, in fact, made Hangzhou. Before 605, Hangzhou was a town with a population of 15,000. However, with the Grand

Canal completed in 610, Hangzhou quickly developed into a cosmopolitan metropolis. By the mid-Tang Dynasty in the eighth century, Hangzhou already had over 30,000 shops.

The amount of commerce and communication along the Grand Canal during the Song Dynasty (960 – 1279), notably the Southern Song (1127 – 1279), triggered global trade with Europe, Africa, and Asia—the very origins of modernity.

### Carved from Time

The 30-minute Grand Canal water trip from the Wulinmen Ferry Terminal to the historic Gongchen Bridge shows how the past and present blend—modern glass towers and apartments as well as small pagodas and statues.

The first part of the Grand Canal was dug in the fifth century BCE in northern China. Its southern terminus in Hangzhou came into being until a thousand years later during the Sui Dynasty. The Emperor Yang of Sui forced millions of workers to stretch the canal first down to Hangzhou, and then northwest to Zhuozhou in present Hebei Province. In four years, the Emperor

cosmopolitan metropolis
国际性的大都市

trigger
激发

origin
起源

modernity
现代性

terminal
终点

blend
混合

come into being
形成

| | |
|---|---|
| at the cost of | built 2,000 kilometers of canals, which was at the cost of many workers. |
| 以……为代价 | |
| attribute to | Though many scholars in the Tang and Song dynasties attributed the downfall of the Sui Dynasty to the building of the Grand Canal, they were also grateful for the project. When it was completed in 610, the canal gave an interior link to five of China's major rivers as well as access to the sea. It contributed to the Golden Era of the Tang and Song dynasties. |
| 归因于 | |
| downfall | |
| 垮台 | |
| grateful | |
| 感谢的 | |
| contribute to | |
| 贡献 | |
| swan song | ## Swan Song |
| 最后的作品 | The Grand Canal truly soared during the Song Dynasty. The population of Hangzhou reached 1.5 million, and the city became best known for her silk and tea. Northern China was also reliant on Hangzhou's grain production. |
| reliant on | |
| 依赖 | |
| ingenious | |
| 有独创性的 | |
| doubt-gate lock | In 984, an ingenious engineer invented the double-gate lock to safeguard the canal from bandits. The locks and tributaries of the Grand Canal still stretch through the city. Here in Hangzhou, these canal-side villages and towns sprang up like fields of mushrooms when the northern areas were destroyed and the capital relocated in 1129. |
| 双门船闸 | |
| tributary | |
| 支流 | |
| spring up | |
| 兴起 | |
| relocate | |
| 迁移 | |

The Grand Canal in Hangzhou during the Song made a deep impression on visitors. For example, two travelers, Ibn Battuta and Marco Polo, each marveled at the Grand Canal when they visited Hangzhou.

In the 1280s, Marco Polo visited the Grand Canal at Hangzhou: "At the back of the market places, there runs a very large canal, on the bank of which towards the squares are built great houses of stone, in which the merchants from India and other foreign parts store their wares, to be handy for the markets," Marco Polo remarked, "In each of the squares is held a market three days in the week, visited by 40,000 or 50,000 persons, who bring there for sale every possible necessity."

**Bridge over Fabled Waters**

Between 1411 and 1415, the canal was expanded with 300,000 laborers dredging it and building a new canal route. This made Suzhou under the influence of the canal, yet left Hangzhou as its primary southern end. In the Ming Dynasty (1368 – 1644), over 120,000 soldiers and officials were dispatched in garrisons along the canal. For centuries,

marvel at
对……惊奇

merchant
商人

ware
制品

handy
方便的

remark
评论

necessity
生活必需品

fabled
传说中的

dredge
疏浚

influence
影响

dispatch
派遣

garrison
要塞

**salute**
致敬

**decorate**
装饰

**inscription**
石刻文字

**course**
河道

**prominence**
重要性

**decrease**
降低

**heritage**
遗产

merchants would mark their journey at the famous Gongchen Bridge.

Indeed, Gongchen Bridge means "Salute to Emperor's Place" and has three moon-shaped arches, decorated with the carvings of two dragons playing with a fire ball, lotuses and inscriptions. In 1855 the Yellow River flooded and changed course, reducing the canal's prominence. Later, railway projects in the early 20th century further decreased its value.

The Grand Canal began to see more traffic after 1949, and today the canal still sees important shipping through Shandong, Jiangsu, and Zhejiang provinces.

As of 2014, the Grand Canal was listed as a UNESCO World Heritage Site, and it's no surprise considering how the Grand Canal shaped the Chinese nation and it is still serving the country.

### Historic Streets

Standing at Gongchen Bridge, one can see the historical importance of this bridge and canal. Covering nearly 80,000 square meters, this was once the main ferry terminal during the

Tongzhi period of the Qing Dynasty (1616 – 1911). Architecture from that time still stands and there are a lot of museums, including museums of fans, umbrellas, knives, scissors, and swords. The umbrella museum in particular is a pleasant surprise; Hangzhou was, after all, the world's capital for silk parasols.

For the perfect stroll along the Grand Canal, visit Xiaohezhi Street. Located at the junction of the Grand Canal, Xiaohe River, and Yuhangtang River, the street flourished as a suburb during the Tang and Song dynasties before becoming a commercial hub in the 20th century. Today it hosts some of the "indigenous dwellers" of the neighborhood along with souvenir shops and cafes.

scissors
剪刀

sword
剑

parasol
阳伞

stroll
漫步

junction
交汇

suburb
郊区

indigenous dweller
原住民

# Xiangji Temple

Opposite to Xiaohezhi Street to the western bank of the Grand Canal, nestled in deep alleyways, is a monastery called Xiangji Temple, notable for being the only one worshiping Kinnara, in Chinese translated as "The Bodhisattva Supervising the Kitchen." Built in 978, it was the first monastery to greet sailors and pilgrims that took the Grand Canal to Hangzhou. For pilgrims' convenience, the waterway directly connected to the temple gate. The present monastery was rebuilt in 2010, featuring a lavish use of copper in its major buildings, including pillars, corridors, the drum tower, and prayer halls. The sole remnant of its former buildings is the pagoda built in 1713.

---

nestle
坐落

monastery
僧院

notable
著名的

worship
崇拜

supervise
主管

convenience
便利

lavish
大量的

pillar
柱子

corridor
走廊

remnant
残余

## Hangzhou's Protector

The people who lived around West Lake became famous too, in particular, after Hangzhou became a Chinese capital. Although the Tang Dynasty collapsed in 907, Hangzhou kept its riches and strategic position. A new political power known as the Wuyue Kingdom rose with Hangzhou as its capital. Later, it came the "Five Dynasties and Ten Kingdoms Period," when several states competed against each other. Then the Song Dynasty unified them in 960.

The Qian family ruled the Wuyue and indeed, the Qian family's influence kept to this day in Hangzhou, with their own family museum, King Qian's Temple, along the eastern bank of West Lake.

The Wuyue Kingdom extended from modern day Shanghai down to Fujian Province. Its capital, Hangzhou, was called Qiantang and became a center for regional commerce. Under the reign of its first king Qian Liu, Buddhism was popular, as were sea-trade and infrastructure. West Lake was dredged

protector
保护者

collapse
瓦解

riches
财富

strategic
战略的

compete
竞争

regional
地区的

reign
统治

| | |
|---|---|
| seawall 海塘 | |
| maritime 海的 | |
| monk 僧侣 | |
| Chan (Zen) Buddhism 禅宗 | |
| flock 蜂拥而至 | |
| landscape 风景 | |
| subdue 征服 | |
| octagonal 八边形的 | |
| subjugate 征服 | |
| recall 召回 | |
| bow 屈服 | |

and the Qiantang River given seawalls, and the kingdom's maritime strength allowed it to develop formal relations with Japan in 935, as well as keep ties with northern Chinese kingdoms and Korea. Therefore, monks of Chan (Zen) Buddhism from Japan and Korea flocked to it to study—with Wuyue monks visiting the temples in Japan and Korea. The Wuyue left two towers on West Lake's landscape. One is the seven-story Baochu Pagoda; Baochu or "Protect Chu" tower was destroyed and rebuilt a few times throughout history, most recently in 1933. The modern one is slightly shorter than the original. Still, it stands above the northern shore of West Lake.

Despite coming to power in 960, it would take 18 years for the Song to totally subdue King Qian Chu. As a last stand of sorts, he built octagonal seven-story Leifeng Pagoda in honor of his newborn son in 975 on the southern shore of West Lake.

The pagoda took two years to complete, and a new Song emperor came to power. Qian Chu was subjugated and recalled to Kaifeng with his court of 3,000. Merely a decade after bowing to the Song, he died in 988 after a birthday celebration. His sons would go on to guide Hangzhou into its greatest years under the Song. King Qian Chu could never have imagined that, over 140 years after his death, his beloved city of Hangzhou would become the capital of the Song, by then known as the Southern Song Dynasty. Through its advanced technology, culture, and communication, his later descendants would manage a city and empire that would alter the course of world history.

advanced
先进的

descendant
后代

alter
改变

## Glowing with Leifeng

glow
发光

finger snap
响指

proclaim
宣称

Buddhist
佛教的

hollowed out
挖空的

sacred
神圣的

ascend
攀登

escalator
电梯

fortress
堡垒

devoted
虔诚的

rotunda
圆形大厅

Hangzhou, like Rome, wasn't built in a day. But Leifeng Pagoda was erected, "within a moment of a finger snap," so proclaims a Buddhist inscription from over 2,000 years ago when the pagoda was first built. Archaeologists found it inside one of the hollowed out sacred Buddhist bricks.

These sacred bricks rest in ruins under the foundations of the current Leifeng Pagoda, which was reconstructed and brought back to its former glory in 2002.

To ascend this octagonal tower, one can climb steps or take an escalator. Once up the hill, the mystery of this pagoda starts to unfold. This was a fortress for sacred Buddhist learning and power. The last ruler of the coastal kingdom of Wuyue in the 10th century, Qian was a devoted Buddhist. Countless pagodas and temples were built during his rule.

Looking at the dusty bricks in the spacious rotunda, one can be reminded of the distant past. Above this floor is the entrance to the glass elevator that propels visitors skyward into the modern pagoda. One sees the breathtaking views of West Lake and will understand why the pagoda holds a place in the Chinese literary imagination.

The magnificent view gave birth to the term "Leifeng Pagoda in Evening Glow," and is among the Top Ten Scenes of West Lake. In the late 16th and early 17th centuries, a legend arose that under the pagoda a white snake demon was trapped because of its love affair with a human. Although this is not a horror story but a heartbreaking romance that made Leifeng Pagoda a symbol for eternal love.

The legend came to famous writer Lu Xun's mind when the pagoda collapsed in 1924. In an article he wrote, the collapse of the pagoda represented the collapse of feudal traditions.

propel
驱使

breathtaking
令人激动的

literary
文学的

magnificent
壮丽的

give birth to
诞生

Leifeng Pagoda in Evening Glow
雷峰夕照

feudal
封建的

## The Legend of the White Snake

Have you ever felt like your wife was hiding something from you? Legendary scholar Xu Xian had that feeling once, too. And it turned out he was right. Xu Xian's wife was hiding the fact that she was actually a snake demon.

The Legend of the White Snake is one of China's most popular old tales; it was passed down orally from history.

Once upon a time, there was a white snake demon named Bai Suzhen. She lived in the land of demons, but desired to become more powerful. She came to the human world and took on the form of a beautiful woman.

While there, she met a green snake demon named Xiao Qing who was causing trouble. The two became close friends and traveled the world together in human form. It was at Hangzhou's beautiful West Lake, on a rainy day by the Broken Bridge, that they met the scholar Xu Xian, who shared a boat with them and let them use his umbrella. Bai fell madly in love with the human, and used her magical power to set up more opportunities for them to meet until they finally married. Karma, it is said, is what drew them together; Xu was a cowherd in a previous life who once saved a small white snake, so the match was destined to be.

Of course, Xu was not aware that his wife was a snake demon. They opened a medicine shop named Bao He Tang together and became widely known for giving away free herbs to people who couldn't afford to pay.

However, a monk named Fahai could see Bai and Qing for what they really were, and he was dedicated to destroying all demons. One year during the Dragon Boat Festival, Xu prepared Bai a special surprise recommended by Fahai: wine filled with herbs that could drive away all demons. Bai drank the wine and immediately turned back into a snake. Her husband, shocked beyond belief, died. Bai returned to human form, obtained some sacred herbs, and brought her husband back to life.

However, Fahai locked Xu away in Jinshan Temple. Bai angrily destroyed the temple, violating the laws of Heaven, and faced timeless imprisonment in the Leifeng Pagoda. But some versions have Xiao Qing, the green snake demon,

---

Karma
因缘

cowherd
放牛娃

be destined
命中注定

give away
赠送

herb
草药

be dedicated to
致力于

drive away
赶走

obtain
取得

violate
违反

imprisonment
囚禁

version
版本

reunite
重聚

dot
点缀

scenic spot
景点

TCM shop
中药店

coming to her help. As such, the story often ends with Bai, her husband, and their son reunited.

The legend of the white snake has stayed with Hangzhou over the years, with stories of the loving couple dotting many scenic spots, from the Broken Bridge and the Leifeng Pagoda to the Bao He Tang TCM shop in Qinghefang. Couples come from all over China to experience the locations of this Hangzhou love story.

## Dawn of the Southern Song

The morning sun warms the face, and the scent of flowers fills the air. Along the Su Causeway are some of the many simple pleasures in which visitors can delight. Named after the poet and official Su Shi, "Spring Dawn at Su Causeway" is the first among the Top Ten Scenes of the lake.

The official Su Shi had West Lake dredged, giving employment to more than 200,000 workers during his time here. This set Hangzhou apart from other cities across China and the world—a balance of nature and city life. Both his work and his literary legacy are the reason the Su Causeway bears his name.

During the Song period's peak, China's population rose quickly from 50 million to 100 million with advances made in chemistry, math, poetry, and worldwide trade, and with that success came a powerful navy and merchant ships which would see the shores of Arabia and India. Over centuries of careful management, Hangzhou rose as one of the major commercial ports of the age.

When the Northern Song capital of

---

scent
气味

delight
享受

Spring Dawn at
Su Causeway
苏堤春晓

peak
顶峰

navy
海军

capture
俘获

ascend to the throne
登上王位

flee
逃亡

refugee
难民

unique
独一无二的

associate with
与……联系

Kaifeng fell to Jurchen invaders of the Jin Dynasty in 1127, emperors and most of the royal family were captured, and the ninth prince Zhao Gou escaped to the south. He ascended to the throne in Nanjing and became the first emperor of Southern Song Dynasty, Emperor Gaozong of Song. In the first few years as an emperor, he spent most of his time fleeing, and at one point was driven to the sea by Jurchen armies and spent four months on a boat.

It wasn't until 1138 that the court was fully established in Hangzhou, and, for the city's protection, thick walls were built all around. With refugees flowing in from the north, the city's population rose quickly. Eventually, the city's southern wall extended over Wushan Hill and north to the Grand Canal, west to the eastern shore of West Lake and east to Qiantang River. Walk around the eastern shore of West Lake and you will find some of the city gate relics. Built in 1148, the relics are protected in glass at Hubin Road and Qingchun Road, just 90 meters from the shores. It had a unique architecture that was typical of Song construction associated with the former capital in Kaifeng.

From the imperial city, an imperial

street, or "heavenly street," run south-north through the city, which is roughly today's Zhongshan Road. Along the road were shops and stores of all kinds that were busy into the night. A section of the original royal street was excavated in 2004 and preserved for modern visitors to see in the Southern Song Relic Museum by the Zhongshan South Road.

Over the following years, Emperor Gaozong devoted much of his time to architecture projects and garden planning inside the imperial city and around town, which formed the Southern Song style. Unfortunately, a mysterious fire in 1277 destroyed the imperial city. What remains today are relics buried underground and a stele of Emperor Gaozong's calligraphy work on the hill.

For a bird's eye view of the glorious capital, head to Hangzhou Museum on Wushan Hill where you can look out over the imperial city or explore the capital through a motion sensing digital exhibition.

stele
碑

calligraphy work
书法作品

bird's eye view
鸟瞰

motion sensing digital exhibition
体感数字展

# Eight-trigram Cropland Park

Shaped like a bagua, or eight trigrams, a symbol to represent the fundamental principles of reality in Daoist cosmology, this farmland was also of imperial importance in the Southern Song Dynasty. The 60,000-square-meter park area now features the octagon farmland surrounded by water channels with different crops of varied colors. The center area takes the shape of a round Taiji, in which Longjing tea and other Hangzhou native crops are planted. The best place to get a bird's eye view of the neat pattern is up on the Jade Emperor Hill in front of the Zilai Cave, a Daoist relic. The park itself is decorated with reliefs of ancient agricultural ceremonies and other exhibitions.

---

bagua
八卦

Daoist cosmology
道教的宇宙观

feature
以……为特点

relief
浮雕

## Discover Song Porcelain

Southern Song porcelain represents the peak of the ancient Chinese art and techniques. Especially well known was Southern Song celadon, also known as "green ware." Light green, gray, or yellow glazed plates, vases, etc. with simple and elegant style—Southern Song porcelain was the empire's major export at the time via the Maritime Silk Road to Southeast Asia, Persia, Europe, and as far as Africa.

Most recently, studies from a sunken ship of late Southern Song named Nanhai One, found near the coast of Guangdong in 2007, revealed more than 60,000 pieces of porcelain. These pieces provided key insights into the porcelain industry and international trade at that time. Most interestingly, some of them were clearly designed for a foreign market, featuring Arabic and other foreign styles, many of which had never been seen by Chinese porcelain experts before. Official porcelain production was at an even higher level, produced for the rich and powerful. Two official kilns, or *guan* kilns, could be found in the historical records of Hangzhou.

---

celadon
青瓷

glazed
上釉的

via
通过

Maritime Silk Road
海上丝绸之路

insight
深刻见解

*guan* kiln
官窑

crackled glaze
裂纹釉

workshop
作坊

　　The Altar of Heaven Kiln was excavated in the 1950s. The Department of Palace Supply Kiln is more mysterious. For decades, no one was able to locate it despite relatively detailed historical records. Some even claim that it didn't exist at all. It wasn't until 1996 that a kiln located between the Phoenix and Jiuhua hills was excavated. Here, archaeologists discovered bits and pieces of powdered blue and crackled glaze that were believed to have been made for the royal family and high officials. Today these pieces can also be seen at the Southern Song Dynasty Guan Kiln Museum which features an original kiln site, exhibition hall of porcelain treasures, and a traditional workshop display.

## West Lake, History, and Tomorrow

In 1276, the city's place as a great Chinese capital ended with the arrival of Kublai Khan's army, but the Southern Song left a legacy of architecture, poetry, and culture that endures to this day.

Gradually, by the Qing Dynasty, all the famous sites so familiar today were in place, thanks in no small part to Qing Emperor Kangxi, who left calligraphy for the Ten Scenic Spots; his grandson Emperor Qianlong wrote a poem for each site. Today, the words of the two emperors are carved in stone on 10 steles at the most memorable sites in Hangzhou.

endure
持续

memorable
值得纪念的

Jixian Pavilion at West Lake

# Marco Polo's City of Heaven

Whether or not the famous Marco Polo was aware of the generation-long battle of the Khan against the Song, he did indeed enjoy the beauty of what remained:..the greatest palace in the world...It is all painted in gold, with many histories and representations of beasts and birds, of knights and ladies, and many marvelous things. It forms a really magnificent sight, for over all the walls and all the ceiling you see nothing but paintings in gold. Referred to as Kinsay in *The Travels of Marco Polo*, Marco Polo said, inside the city there is a lake which is some 30 miles and all round it are built beautiful palaces and houses, of the richest and most delicate structure that you can imagine, belonging to the nobles of the city. Of the people, he called the "men and women fair and comely," remarking on the bridges, sugar, and silk of this Asian land of plenty. "When they return home they say they have been to Kinsay or the City of Heaven, and their only desire is to get back as soon as possible."

knight
骑士

delicate
精美的

noble
贵族

comely
好看的

reliable
可靠的

omit
省略

landmark
地标

inspect
调查

revenue
收入

enthusiastically
热情地

toman
古波斯金币

for the sake of
为了

hospitality
好客

entertain
款待

## Polo and Prosperity

Now, it must be said that Marco Polo is far from a reliable source—omitting lots of both history and landmarks in his travels, and claiming at one point that Hangzhou had pears of over 10 pounds. In the end, however, this wasn't a vacation; Marco Polo was sent by the Great Khan to inspect the revenue brought in by the land south of the Yellow River. The salt alone caused the Venetian traveler to praise Hangzhou enthusiastically: "[Salt makes] eighty tomans of gold...In fact, a vast sum of money!" He spoke of the various items that came through that great port of industry and trade—of the rice wine, the Indian traders, the tradesmen, the silk. "They also treat the foreigners who visit them for the sake of trade with great hospitality, and entertain them in the most charming manner, giving them every help and advice on their business."

## The Civilized Song

It was with the people of Kinsay that Marco Polo was so impressed. To him, this City of Heaven seemed like the most civilized place he had yet visited in his travels in the Khan's kingdom.

Of the nature of the men of Hangzhou, he said, "The natives of the city are men of peaceful character, both from education and from the example of their kings…They know nothing of using arms, and keep none in their houses. You hear of no noisy quarrels of any kind among them." The women, to him, seemed some of the most elegant in the world, adorned in silks and fine perfumes. As for the people: "They are thoroughly honest and truthful, and there is such a degree of good will and neighborly relation among both men and women that you would take the people who live in the same street to be all one family."

native
本地人

adorn
装饰

perfume
香气

thoroughly
完全地

neighborly
睦邻

# The Butterfly Effect at Wansong Academy

It's a legend of love and learning—the "Butterfly Lovers," or "Liang Zhu," one of the most well-known romantic folk legends of China. Having been passed down for almost 1,700 years across different regions of China, the story has been made into countless movies, plays, operas, and even a concerto. Hangzhou played a special role: it's the place where the couple in the story fell in love.

The story begins with the wealthy daughter, Zhu Yingtai, gaining entry to a famous academy—a place dominated by men. This was the Wansong Academy, founded in 1498 in southeastern Hangzhou at Phoenix Hill. Zhu disguises herself as a boy and meets another student, Liang Shanbo. The two become fast friends and in the three years of study, Zhu secretly falls in love with Liang. Liang is blind to Zhu's secret love, and, of course, the fact that she is female. Then Zhu is suddenly called back home.

It is said that the two friends couldn't bear to part from each other, so they traveled together for 18 *li* (9 kilometers) before saying goodbye. The pair crossed the same bridge on West Lake back and forth 18 times, giving it the name "Long Bridge" or Changqiao. Zhu hints several times during this journey that she loves Liang. She even promises to match Liang with her "sister" for marriage. Months pass and Liang pays a visit to Zhu's hometown where it is finally made clear that she is a woman; the two fall madly in love. But, their love is not to be, as Zhu finds she is to be married to a rich playboy. The news is such a blow to Liang and his health begins to fail—finally leading to his tragic death.

On the day of Zhu's wedding, a strong wind stops her marriage procession from passing where Liang is buried. She steps out of the sedan to pay her respects. There, the ground opens and she jumps into it to join Liang in his grave. The ground closes and two butterflies appear as their spirits, dancing in the wind, never again to be parted.

Originally equipped with a full library, scientific instruments, and a school of management, the Wansong Academy was visited by Qing Dynasty emperors Kangxi and Qianlong, both of whom left calligraphy there. Although it declined

---

hint
暗示

blow
打击

tragic
悲剧的

procession
队伍

sedan
轿子

equip with
配备

decline
衰落

**fitting**
适合的

**matchmaking**
相亲

in the early 20th century, the buildings have been brought back to their Ming glory.

And, to some extent, the legend of the "Butterfly Lovers" has a fitting memorial here; April hosts floral festivals and May sees a matchmaking event at the campus—honoring the love between Zhu and Liang in their student days.

## Historical Hotspots

Hangzhou has more than just West Lake's waters; one can barely walk a block around the lake without coming across a historical site. The most efficient way to catch a glimpse of this long and fascinating past is to visit one of the concentrations of historical hotspots, which can be found on and around Gushan Hill, the island located near the northern side of West Lake, connected to the shore by Xiling Bridge on the west and Bai Causeway on the east.

### Temple of Yue Fei

A great place to start with is the warrior poet Yue Fei, whose tomb and temple is located on the shore just a few minutes' walk west from the Xiling Bridge entrance to Gushan Hill.

It's not an exaggeration to say that most Chinese have heard the tale of this determined general who was skilled at arms, loyal to the crown and saw the growing threat from northern invaders and who died at the treachery of the royal chancellor Qin Hui.

---

hotspot
热点

concentration
聚集地

exaggeration
夸张

treachery
背叛

chancellor
大臣

| | |
|---|---|
| tattoo | |
| 刺青 | |

| | |
|---|---|
| as opposed to | |
| 与……截然相反 | |

| | |
|---|---|
| thread | |
| 线索 | |

| | |
|---|---|
| strangle | |
| 勒死 | |

| | |
|---|---|
| execute | |
| 处死 | |

Perhaps most of all, Chinese have heard the tales of the four-character tattoo said to be on Yue Fei's back, 精忠报国, which means, "serve the country with strong loyalty."

Most tales say Yue Fei joined the military at a young age. His bravery and skills drew attention and he worked his way up in the Southern Song army. So when the Jurchen invaders from the north invaded his homeland, he was among those most eager to take up the fight.

And fight he did, winning plenty of battles. So much so that Yue Fei became a symbol of continuing the fight, as opposed to his political enemy Qin Hui, who was pushing for peace with the northern invaders.

The tales differ on exactly how Qin Hui brought Yue Fei down, but a common thread is that while Yue Fei was on the battlefield, Qin Hui was saying bad words about Yue Fei at court. The common theme of Yue Fei's death is treachery at the hands of Qin Hui, but in some tales, he was strangled, and in others, he was poisoned, executed, dying in prison—the list goes on.

War against the Jurchen continued

and the troubles with the north were far from over at the time of Yue Fei's death. History proved his suspicion of the northern invaders correct—they had no interest in peace. Around 20 years after Yue Fei died, it was time for Qin Hui to go on the chopping block. Yue Fei was given a grand tomb and is remembered to this day. Visitors to the tomb should definitely make sure they take the time to see the kneeling statues in one of the courtyard areas. There they will find in an enclosure, a kneeling stone figure of Qin Hui beside his wife, looking every bit as miserable as one would expect from a bad man who will soon be executed.

## Xiling Seal Engravers' Society

Once across Xiling Bridge, you can begin exploring Gushan Hill, a quiet small island that was favored by literary recluses for centuries.

The southern side of the island has a road and buildings; on the north there is mostly parkland. If you start your trip on the road-covered side, you will immediately come across the former house of Chinese scholar Yu Yue. Passing through it and out the

suspicion
怀疑

chopping block
砧板

kneel
跪着

enclosure
围栏

miserable
悲惨的

recluse
隐士

parkland
有草木的开阔地

representative
代表

school
流派

negative space
留白

a stone's throw from
离……非常近

wander
漫步

impressively
令人难忘地

back of the house, is one of many short, charming stone paths that allow visitors to get to the top of the peak (in just a few short minutes) and find themselves amid the buildings used by the Xiling Seal Engravers' Society. There visitors can see plenty of seals painted on the walls, representative of the various seal schools that existed throughout China.

The society was founded in 1904, when various seal groups from across China came together to form the one united society. The history of each school dates back to the Qing and Ming dynasties. It's easy to see the differences between the different styles of seal; one can find some of the differences between the "yin and yang" styles—whether the character is pressed from the ink, or can be seen in the negative space that lacks ink.

### Delights of Gushan Hill

Just a stone's throw from the palace lies the Zhejiang Provincial Museum. Here, amid the cool stone blocks, visitors can wander through impressively large collections of ancient porcelain, catch a glimpse into how aspects of Han culture developed over thousands of years, and gain an insight into the relics across the wider Zhejiang area.

On the west of museum's main hall, you will find a beautiful garden of courtyard of pavilions, corridors, pools, bridges, and artificial rockeries. Called Wenlan Pavilion, it is a famous imperial library built during the period of Emperor Qianlong. The proudest collection in this library is *Complete Library in Four Branches of Literature*, the largest encyclopedia in the world at the time. In a fire in 1861, the old library building was destroyed and part of the book lost. Over the years, local scholars recompiled it and copies were gradually restored to bring this collection back to its former glory.

Before you finish the trip around the island, visit the northern side. Amid the parkland and the statue of literary genius Lu Xun, visitors can find a number of monuments to literary wisdom, including the home of Lin Bu, a poet of the Northern Song Dynasty and lover of cranes and plum flowers.

---

artificial rockery
假山

*Complete Library in Four Branches of Literature*
《四库全书》

encyclopedia
百科全书

recompile
重新汇编

genius
天才

monument
历史遗迹

crane
鹤

plum flower
梅花

# Appendix

## Place Names 地名机构名对照表

Altar of Heaven Kiln 郊坛下官窑

Bai Causeway 白堤

Bao He Tang 保和堂

Baochu Pagoda 保俶塔

Baoshi Hill 宝石山

Broken Bridge 断桥

Department of Palace Supply Kiln 修内司官窑

Drum Tower 鼓楼

Eight-trigram Cropland Park 八卦田遗址公园

Fanshan Hill 反山

Gongchen Bridge 拱宸桥

Gushan Hill 孤山

Hangzhou Arts and Crafts Museum 杭州工艺美术博物馆

Hangzhou Museum 杭州博物馆

Jade Emperor Hill 玉皇山

Jinshan Temple 金山寺

Jiuhua Hill 九华山

King Qian's Temple 钱王祠

Kuahuqiao Site Museum 跨湖桥遗址公园

Kuaiji Hill 会稽山

Leifeng Pagoda 雷峰塔

Liangzhu Museum 良渚博物院

Long Bridge Park 长桥公园

Morocco 摩洛哥

Pearl River 珠江

Persia 波斯

Phoenix Hill 凤凰山

Qiantang 钱塘

Qiantang County 钱唐县

Qiantang River 钱塘江

Qinghefang 清河坊

South China Sea 南海

Southern Song Dynasty Guan Kiln Museum 南宋官窑博物馆

Southern Song Relic Museum 南宋遗址陈列馆

Su Causeway 苏堤

Suzhou 苏州

Temple/Mausoleum of Yue Fei 岳王庙/墓

Temple of Yu Qian 于谦祠

The Grand Canal 大运河

The Grand Jing-Hang Canal Museum 中国京杭大运河博物馆

UNESCO 联合国教科文组织

UNESCO World Heritage Site
联合国教科文组织世界文化遗产

Venice 威尼斯

Wangxian Pavilion 望仙阁

Wansong Academy 万松书院

Wenlan Pavilion 文澜阁

West Lake 西湖

Wulinmen Ferry Terminal 武林门码头

Wushan Hill 吴山

Wuyue Kingdom 吴越国

Xiangguo Well 相国井

Xianghu Lake 湘湖

Xiangji Temple 香积寺

Xiaohe River 小河

Xiaohezhi Street 小河直街

Xiaoshan District 萧山区

Xiling Bridge 西泠桥

Xiling Seal Engravers' Society 西泠印社

Xixi Wetlands 西溪湿地

Yangtze River 长江

Yellow River 黄河

Yuhang District 余杭区

Yuhangtang River 余杭塘河

Zhejiang Provincial Museum
浙江省博物馆

Zhuozhou 涿州

Zhongshan Park 中山公园

Zilai Cave 紫来洞

## Names of Important Figures 人名对照表

Bai Juyi 白居易

Bai Suzhen 白素贞

Emperor Gaozong of Song
宋高宗

Emperor Kangxi 康熙皇帝

Emperor Qianlong 乾隆皇帝

Emperor Taizong of Tang 唐太宗

Emperor Yang of Sui 隋炀帝

Fahai 法海

Hua Xin 华信

Ibn Battuta 伊本 · 白图泰

King Fuchai of Wu 吴王夫差

King Goujian of Yue 越王勾践

Kinnara 紧那罗菩萨

Kublai Khan 忽必烈汗

Li Bi 李泌

Liang Shanbo 梁山伯

Lin Bu 林逋

Lu Xun 鲁迅

Marco Polo 马可 · 波罗

Qian Chu 钱俶

Qian Liu 钱镠

Qin Hui 秦桧

Qin Shi Huang 秦始皇

Su Shi 苏轼

Wu Zixu 伍子胥

Xiao Qing 小青

Xishi (Xizi) 西施（西子）

Xu Xian 许仙

Yu the Great 大禹

Yu Yue 俞樾

Yue Fei 岳飞

Zhao Gou 赵构

Zhu Yingtai 祝英台

**图书在版编目 (CIP) 数据**

杭州一瞥：精编版.访古探幽：英文
蒋景阳主编；徐雪英，闻人行编. — 北京：商务印书馆，2023
ISBN 978-7-100-22540-3

Ⅰ.①杭… Ⅱ.①蒋… ②徐… ③闻… Ⅲ.①英语－语言读物
②旅游指南－杭州－英文 Ⅳ.①H319.4：K

中国国家版本馆CIP数据核字(2023)第102975号

**权利保留，侵权必究。**

**杭州一瞥：精编版**

蒋景阳 主编

商 务 印 书 馆 出 版
（北京王府井大街36号 邮政编码100710）
商 务 印 书 馆 发 行
北京博海升彩色印刷有限公司印刷
ISBN 978-7-100-22540-3

| 2023 年 7 月第 1 版 | 开本 889×1194 1/32 |
|---|---|
| 2023 年 7 月第 1 次印刷 | 印张 7 |

定价：98.00 元